Prior Service Military and Entering the Legal Profession: Financial Issues, Education Benefits and More

Jeffery Ryan Ray, Esq.

LLM Candidate, University of Aberdeen

Juris Doctor (J.D.), Florida A&M University

Post Graduate Program in Human Rights Law, University of Oxford

B.S., Troy University

A.S., Troy University

(Former U.S. Army Sergeant, 13F/Forward Observer at Fort Campbell, Ky/101st Airborne/Air Assault)

The author wishes to express his gratitude to his wife, children, family and friends for their support throughout my experience during law school and thereafter. My wife has been the keystone in my life.

ABSTRACT

This book is an information guide for prior service members that are seeking to become an attorney or enter the legal profession in general. Information that should be considered before making the jump will be invaluable. Citations included are intended to shorten this book and make it more reader friendly. If the reader desires additional information, then the citations provide links that access significant information.

The information contained within was obtained through personal experience and research. Emphasis was placed upon the difficulties of the overall process of entering and proceeding through law school in order to establish the reality of a glorified system. This book demonstrates that prior service members, and others, should think carefully about whether they should go to law school. If the service member decides to proceed, then this guide provides information regarding the process. General information about education benefits and a few suggestions intended to help during law school are included.

CHAPTER I: WHO SHOULD READ AND WHERE DO YOU START

The Audience

This book is intended for military service members for a variety of reasons. The writing style is slightly adapted to use jargon that prior military members, especially US Army veterans, are more likely appreciate. Substantive material is included regarding benefits particular to military veterans. The benefits system is convoluted and in some cases requires some strategy to successfully navigate. Also, this book is intended to assist a group of people that generally get little functional or concrete guidance on career development as they leave the military. However, the roadmap in this book is generally applicable and usable by anyone that wishes to become a lawyer or obtain Juris Doctor (J.D.) credentials needed for many professional fields.

There are many professional fields that may benefit from J.D. credentials. The most obvious vocation is that of the attorney. The State Department actively recruits from law schools around the country and they have diplomats in residence to various universities.[1] Intelligence analysts are recruited from law schools. Would you like to work for the Central Intelligence Agency (CIA)[2], the National Security Agency (NSA)[3], Defense Intelligence agency (DIA)[4], the United Nations (UN)[5], Department of Justice (DoJ)[6], or one of many

---

[1] United States Department of State, Careers Representing America, 'Diplomats in Residence Location Map' <http://careers.state.gov/engage/dir.html> accessed 10 January 2013

[2] Central Intelligence Agency, 'Career Opportunities' <https://www.cia.gov/careers/opportunities/analytical/view-jobs.html> accessed 9 January 2013

[3] National Security Agency, Central Security Service, 'Careers' <http://www.nsa.gov/careers/career_fields/intela.shtml> accessed 9 January 2013

[4] Defense Intelligence Agency, 'Careers' <http://www.dia.mil/careers/> accessed 9 January 2013

[5] United Nations, 'Careers' <https://careers.un.org/lbw/Home.aspx> accessed 9 January 2013

[6] United States Department of Justice, 'Legal Careers' <http://www.justice.gov/careers/legal/> accessed 9 January 2013

other programs that require a legal or analytical background? How about a political career in the legislative branch of a state or federal government? Perhaps the ability to go out on your own and have a boutique law firm is the perfect match for you. Maybe you have an established business and desire to have a greater understanding of the legal background before you expand. Any or all of these reasons benefit by obtaining the J.D. credential. The jobs mentioned above are not an all-inclusive list and may require long hours, the ability to move to the job or many years of building your resume and no guarantee of success. Are you still interested?

The general point thus far has been to establish that there are incredible opportunities out there that a J.D. does prime you for. However, and it is a big however, there is no guarantee and in fact the odds are not in your favor even though you will put in many years of diligent study and pecuniary investment (money pit). Later we will address the dilemma regarding your military benefits and funding along with student loan opportunities. For now, you are merely going to get a taste of the overall cost that you are likely to incur.

Law School may cost you up to 'nearly $60,000' per year at a top-tier law school.[7] After three years of law school, you may end up with a hefty bill—I'll let you do the math. Wait! Did you think about the cost of living? Yes, that is right, the above figure does not include lodging, food, entertainment or other expenses. You will also need extra money to attend internships, conventions related to the field you wish to enter and membership fees in related organizations. However, costs of most state universities are substantially lower than $60,000 per year. In fact, tuition at Florida A&M University, College of Law for the 2012-2013 academic year, was about $14,131.66 for Florida Residents.[8] Tuition for the University of Kentucky, College of law for the 2012-2013 academic year, was about $18,338 for in state tuition.[9] If your eyes are not entirely

---

[7] Business Insider: Law and Order, 'The 20 Most Expensive Law Schools in America' (2012) accessed 9 January 2013

[8] Florida A&M University, College of Law, Prospective Students, 'Tuition and Fees' <http://www.law.famu.edu/go.cfm/do/Page.View/pid/18/t/Tuition-and-Fees> accessed 9 January 2013

[9] University of Kentucky, College of Law, Tuition and Residency, 'Tuition, Fees and Expenses' <http://www.law.uky.edu/index.php?pid=154> accessed 9 January 2013

glossed over by this point, then there is hope.

Are you still interested in pursuing a law degree? You have been warned that the path will be long and onerous. The costs of a law degree, even with your benefits are likely to be significant. If you are still motivated then you are part of the audience that this book is intended for.

The Beginning

The moment you realize that you want to have a professional career is a key point in your life. That point in time will be the beginning of your story and you take a moment to appreciate the beginning of your professional journey. After your head passes through the grand ideas or images of yourself closing the door to your dream home or driving your dream car or insert fantasy desire <here>, then you have some thinking to do. Perhaps the most practical point that should be considered next is whether you know what you are getting yourself into.

Depending on your previous education and military background will largely determine how difficult this path will be for you. Having earned a Bachelor of Science (B.S.) or a Bachelor of Arts (B.A.) prior to the decision to become an attorney will mean that your path will be four years shorter than those of you that have not started progress on a B.S. or B.A. degree. However, even those with a four-year degree still have at least three years of educational requirements, obtaining a J. D., before you can sit for most state bar exams.[10]

For those that have no college background, they have about seven years of university study before meeting the educational qualifications to sit for most bar exams. You must also take a competitive Law School Admissions Test (LSAT), which will be used *inter alia* (look this phrase up in a dictionary if you do not recognize it) in conjunction with your undergraduate grade point average (GPA) for law schools to evaluate you and determine if you are suitable or competitive enough for their institution.

---

[10] American Bar Association, Section of Legal Education and Admissions to the Bar, 'Basic Overview'
<http://www.americanbar.org/groups/legal_education/resources/bar_admissions/basic_over view.html> accessed 9 January 2013

The LSAT is an extremely important portion piece of your law school hopes—take it seriously and take it early. The LSAT test dates will be attainable on the Law School Admission Council's (LSAC) website. Each individual law school has its own deadline for applications, mark them on your calendar and apply early. Make sure that you have your LSAT scores and completed application ready soon after the school indicates it is accepting applications for the next academic term.

Commercial LSAT programs exist in order to help you maximize your LSAT scores, for a fairly substantial fee. Give yourself enough time to take the LSAT a second time if you do not achieve your desired results. This may be the difference between getting into law school and having to repeat the process over entirely the following year. The LSAC has a calculator to help you evaluate where you stand regarding competitiveness against most, if not all, U.S. law schools.

For those readers that do not have substantial funds for a primer course in preparation for the LSAT, do not lose hope. Some of you will have a natural propensity toward thinking in a logic-based manner. Others can obtain an LSAT study guide from a commercial retailer or online site such as Amazon.com.

The selection process is a small glimpse into the convoluted, but highly interesting, world of law school. The journey will be long, much like a marathon. Take a few days to think about whether to move forward with this because the complicated process will become further complicated as you progress.

Deciding to move forward will take great effort in and of itself. One can embark upon a legal career and fail to head in the correct direction and either not be competitive or have spent far too much money for what you wanted in return. Importance surrounding preparation for law school will be discussed later. For now, the gist will be that you will put in far more effort than simply deciding to move forward. If you have a goal in mind, then you must plan for it or likely fall short of your potential.

Have you lost interest at this point? If so, then you will be pleased to know that you found this pearl of wisdom before you spent years of your life and a massive amount of funds in arriving at the decision to waive off from this occupational path. For those of you that are prepared to go all-in on this endeavor, then we start the journey through this brief book and strive to prepare you for the difficulties to come. Perhaps a cup of coffee, tea or whiskey would be a good endeavor to settle down before moving on.

CHAPTER II: FAMILY AND FRIENDS

Family

Obtaining a law degree is like running a marathon. The process is very long, very difficult and you must keep a constant effort throughout the entire ordeal. Unfortunately, you are not the only person affected by this choice. Whether you are single, married, have children or some combination thereof, the dynamics of your relationship with family are likely to change if you embark upon this journey.

A discussion with your family prior to beginning the process will likely help you manage this relationship shift, to a degree, by providing awareness that a change is likely on the horizon. Some law schools have a family orientation event that is a response to the issues that arise between law students and their family whilst attending the three-year programs.[11]

---

[11] Capital University, Law School, 'Family Support Services' <http://law.capital.edu/Family_Support_Services/> accessed 9 January 2013

Even when providing family with advanced notice you can expect push-back from them when you are on a spring or fall break. Law students will be reading and writing for an assignment due a week or two after returning to law school instead of spending the majority of that time with family. The actual intensity of the program will be something that you cannot truly convey in words that will be fully appreciated. The overall goal is to exit the J.D. program with your preexisting relationship(s) intact.

Drama much? The preceding paragraph may seem like an over reaction until the day you hand in your first, and hopefully last, Bar Exam. Be prepared to owe your family member(s) a massive backlog of emotional, physical, moral and perhaps spiritual support. You may be thinking that you can internalize much of what is expected from you during those three years and you will, after all, be physically present and able to help out when you get the chance. If you thought that, then you have missed the point of how and what you may owe your family.

Think of your family offering you a moral and emotional support credit card upon entering law school. Your moral, physical or emotional absences will accumulate during your law school career. It is not the positive withdraw of support that you must worry about. It is the absence of your contributions to the family dynamics that passively requires family members to absorb or fill in and thereby accumulating a debt that will become due at some point.

A great deal of your "credit limit" can be discussed responsibly upfront. Care must be taken to steer away from telling your family that will buy them X, Y or Z once you begin practicing law. There is no guarantee that you will pass law school, the Bar Exam or make a high salary if you accomplish all of these goals. The issue is compounded if you have children.

The difficulties of attending law school when you have children are particular and extensive. Analogizing it to an absent parent would not be far from the truth of the matter.[12] Care must be taken to plan around a long schedule of classes, study, research, writing and editing materials. The difficulty balancing responsibilities regarding children and law school are highly acute when you are the sole provider.

There were single parents that I went to law school with. A few single parents made it through the grueling gauntlet with me. The number of single parents that successfully passed the Florida Bar Exam thereafter was less. This is not an effort to dissuade single parents from attending law school. However, thought must be given to the minimum 8-12 hours per day that you will likely spend on your new endeavor. Then you must account for the study period for the Bar Exam.

Bar Exam study will consume massive amounts of time and you will likely have no income from student loans, scholarships or military educational benefits. More information will follow on the financial problems of the Bar Exam in a later chapter. Shuffling your schedule to take care of your law school responsibilities and your family responsibilities will reserve all of your time, most of the time.[13]

---

[12] Associate's Mind, 'How to Juggle a Family and Law School (or a Law Firm)' <http://associatesmind.com/2011/06/23/how-to-juggle-a-family-and-law-school-or-a-law-firm/> accessed 9 January 2013

[13] Ibid

The benefit of a properly prepared family is that you have an invaluable support resource. A spouse, parent or sibling could provide moral, spiritual or financial support whist you study. The general key is awareness for you and those that you care about. This section had a recurring theme of awareness and transparency. The redundancy is intentional and still, likely, understates the problems that can occur.

Friends

The situation with your pre-law school friends is likely to become tenuous or detached to a degree. Think of the typical time spent with friends on a given evening or event. Whether you are involved in a baseball league, weekend fishing, weekly night out in the town, a movie day or just hanging out. Your available time to spend with your friends becomes a form of liquidated currency of time that you will spend quickly in order to compete in law school.

If you spend time with friends often and you have a spouse or children, then the choice may very well be that one of the three must be relinquished. You must take care of your family, so it will likely boil down to your time with friends or being competitive in law school. Sound a little extreme? The dynamics of these relationships will be clear, or at least more so, once the structure of law school grades are explained in a later chapter.

The relationship dynamics become more difficult when you make friends at the law school. This is not to say that you throw away your old friends for new ones. The issue is more complicated. You will need someone to grow with in law school. There will come a time when it takes you arguing with your law school battle-buddy for hours on a topic before either of you understand the underlying information.

The value of a law school battle-buddy cannot be overstated. My experience in law school found that military affiliated people found each other within the first two days of the program—most were acquainted by lunch on the first day. My battle-buddy was the person that held me accountable to him for keeping up in the classes and vice versa. The importance, usefulness and versatility of a law school battle-buddy cannot be overstated.

In considering becoming a law school student, you should understand that the relationship dynamics of most of your friends are likely to change. Talking about the potential change with your friends may be more difficult than discussing the issue with your family. Be careful on how you phrase the discussion. Assuring your friends that you are not preemptively removing them from your 'friend list' could be beneficial but difficult depending on your approach, this is not Facebook nor should it be treated as such. However, they should know that you will soon have a significant drain on your time and your family will likely fill most of the time that you will have left over. The good news is that you will have periods of time that you can surface the law school waters and breathe or live life as you remember.

Family and Friend Time

Now that you have endured the negative sections of this chapter there is hope at the end of the tunnel. Similar to a military deployment, there is a long period of work followed by the hope of a short mid-tour leave. During law school you will have summer and winter breaks that you will have a portion of time to spend time with family and to visit your friends.

The above analogy regarding deployments and law school should be examined. Just as the mid-tour leave is not necessarily granted or allowed, your entire summer break may be spent on an intense project, an internship at a local or distant location, attending classes or even writing a thesis. Time management is a key factor in this aspect of law school.

Time management is, fortunately, a skill that prior military are already equipped with. If you have a spouse, children or friends that you spend significant time with, then those time management skills will be utilized. Time management is also a skill that you should think about when writing your personal statement seeking admission to a law school.

Adequate attention paid to this chapter may reduce your likelihood of incurring substantial relationship damage with your spouse, family or friend. As you progress through the J.D. program, there will be instances where their support will be extraordinarily fulfilling. One such instance of fulfillment is graduation from law school. Three years of commitment, sacrifice and tens of thousands of pages later you have a day that will be forever etched into your mind and your family and/or friends will help to make that a special day, assuming you prepare and manage them appropriately.

CHAPTER III: FINANCE AND PREPARATION

Short-Term Financial Death

Are you looking to become an attorney to make the big bucks? Have you imagined yourself driving an exotic car that you purchase with the proceeds from your first major case? Unless, you have a wealthy family, a substantial savings/investment portfolio or substantial connections in the legal field, then you should research your current endeavor more closely.

The starting salary is statistically more likely to be closer to $40,000 than over $100,000.[14] The cost of obtaining a J.D. is high, just under $120,000 for Florida A&M University, College of Law.[15] Why would anybody accept this short-term financial death? Is it accurate to categorize this as "short-term" financial death or is it more accurately medium to long-term financial death? If you are attending law school for the right reasons, then the answer is that it doesn't matter as much.

---

[14] The New York Times, Business Day, 'The Two-Track Lawyer Market' (26 July 2010) <http://economix.blogs.nytimes.com/2010/07/26/the-two-track-lawyer-

Are you wondering if this author should take his temperature or see a shrink about now? The crux of the preceding paragraph is to illustrate that the average person entering the legal profession should do so because they have a passion or 'a calling', as a favorite professor of mine has described this issue. While this quote is highly applicable to the financial perspectives of undertaking a J.D. program, it is interchangeable in various aspects of law school and life thereafter.

market/> accessed 9 January 2013

[15] Florida A&M University (n 8) [Tuition rates for 2012-2013 rounded up to the next thousand added to the cost of living fees multiplied by the three year full-time program requirement.]

The 'right reasons' will simply be that you have a passion or desire to practice law. Perhaps you have a desire to help battered women. Maybe you want to protect peoples First Amendment rights. Lawyers are needed to advocate for the environment. Maybe you have a desire to practice in the area of armed conflict. Regardless of what area of law that you desire to go into, as long as there is a desire to perform the job function, then you are in the game for the right reason. Are the numbers still ringing in your head? There are various ways to mitigate the financial damage in attending law school.

One of the most obvious methods of debt mitigation during law school is to not have to pay your tuition—scholarships. Most universities have some scholarship program. Do not limit your enquiry about scholarships to just the school. There are potential opportunities in various areas of the community and government.

If you want to enter a specific field, then search the web to see if there is a scholarship for people that want to break into that field.[16] Individual law schools have missions that they seek to operate by. One possibility is for you to scour the various law schools to find one that matches your personal demographics, lineage, life experience or any other part of your life to their law school mission. When you find such a match, then you are likely to have a fair opportunity in being competitive for a scholarship.

---

[16] The Federal Circuit Bar Association, Bench & Bar, 'The Scholarship Series' <http://www.fedcirbar.org/olc/pub/LVFC/cpages/misc/scholar.jsp> accessed 9 January 2013

When discussing scholarships the issue of GPA is likely to come up. Do not shy away from applying to a scholarship simply because you have some preconceived notion that you do not have a competitive GPA. GPAs are relative, even in the realm of law school. If you are attending or applying to a high-ranking institution, then your inherent inclination to needing a higher GPA is more likely to be correct. On the other hand, if you are applying to a mid-tier or newly accredited law school, then the GPA levels are not as competitive. Some schools list general academic profiles for you to have an independent gauge of your relative position in a highly competitive process. If you obtained your degree whilst often being required to attend field exercises, then you may be breathing a sigh of relief.

If you worked or served in the military as you obtained your B.S. or B.A., then your experiences may make up for a reduction that occurred in your GPA. Regarding individual law school scholarships, the non-traditional nature of working whilst obtaining your four-year degree may score you some extra points depending on the program and the essay you submit.

Rising from the Financial Darkness

There is good news to the financial dynamics of entering the legal profession. Medium to long-term annual income can be substantial and in some areas of legal practice the potential income is not capped. Right about now you may be rolling your eyes or expressing disbelief. The honest answer is that there is a substantial chance that even in your medium to long term legal career that you will continue to make $40,000-$70,000 even with a certification as a licensed attorney.

To get a good picture of this, I suggest that you look up the State Attorney's Office (SAO) near you and view the pay scale for new and veteran attorneys. The SAO is a respectable position and provides a wealth of experience for legal practitioners. Unfortunately, you will not become wealthy by working for your state government as a prosecutor. This is not the only legal practice or legally related job that will have a relatively low pay scale that is capped.

This is where long-term strategy provides insight as to why you should take income-capped employment such as the SAO. Four to five years of working for an organization that provides substantial experience and an opportunity to make solid contacts and will prepare attorneys to transition toward a higher income with no cap. Therefore, your financial breakthrough may, and in all likelihood will, require you to create an experience base before obtaining a proper opportunity for financial freedom. This is assuming you desire to take the risk of going out on your own. Many people enjoy a structured life that is stable regardless of pay.

If you enjoy the stability of employment such as the SAO there is still hope of financial security. Some organizations provide a student loan repayment incentive. As you are performing a public service opportunity, then you may have a percentage of your loans paid off as you work. These options are not guaranteed and may be competitive in nature. Another option is loan forgiveness.

Yes, you read that correctly. There is the possibility that you have a large portion of your loans forgiven. One option is 10 years of public service whilst making 120 monthly payments.[17] Now would be an appropriate time for considering if you are willing to struggle through 10 years of income-capped employment to have your loans forgiven. If you desire to work in public service, then the answer is much easier or even a no-brainer. What if you want to take a chance make it big or bust and are concerned that you will not be able to meet the student loan payments?

---

[17] FinAid, The Smart Student Guide to Financial Aid, 'Public Service Loan Forgiveness' <http://www.finaid.org/loans/publicservice.phtml> accessed 10 January 2013

When venturing away from public service there are other student loan options. Income-contingent and income-based loans can help adjust your payments to match your income. These forms of repayment also have the potential for the remainder of your student loan balance to be forgiven after 25 years of repayment.[18] When the debt balance of student loans for law students can easily reach $200,000, or more, balance forgiveness can be substantial especially considering interest accrual and the potential for reduced payments.

---

[18] Ibid

Military Benefits

This is a simple matter that is often convoluted in ways that are difficult to imagine. Depending on your period of service, your primary benefits will be the Montgomery GI Bill (MGIB), the Post 9/11 GI Bill, Veterans Education Assistance Program, Survivors and Dependents Educational Assistance, Veterans Retraining Assistance Program, and other programs.[19] This section is not intended to be an exhaustive explanation of your benefits. The programs are laid out well on the Veterans Affairs (VA) website. The point of this section is to provide you with awareness of available funding and some advice on the use of that funding.

---

[19] United States Department of Veterans Affairs, Benefits, 'Post 9/11 GI Bill & Other Programs' <http://www.gibill.va.gov/benefits/other_programs/dea.html> accessed 10 January 2013

The first note that should be made is that the timeline that the VA operates on is flexible. Your financial woes will not prompt your university or the VA to process the your benefits swiftly. Ensure that you are able to financially hold over for at least 30 days and as close to 60 days as possible without defaulting on financial obligations. This is difficult for most people. Obtaining a credit line or credit card that you can use may substitute for cash reserves as needed. Care must be taken not to over indulge as that safety net may be needed several times during law school and when studying for the Bar Exam or waiting for the Bar Exam results and looking for employment.

Student loans may provide a time bridge until your benefits kick in or even supplement your military benefits. If needed, you could take out some student loans to provide a larger reserve should the VA have an issue with processing your funds. Of course, we all know that the US Government is always efficient and effective when starting or stopping payments. Whether you should and to what degree you need a cash reserve is a matter for you to determine.

A matter that is particular to the MGIB and Post 9/11 GI Bill (Post 9/11) is the potential for conversion from MGIB to the Post 9/11. This process is not necessarily in your favor to initiate immediately. In fact, the conversion should be carefully weighed as your specific factual situation may change the level of benefit to you or even make it a disadvantage for you. MGIB pays you monthly a flat rate of $1,564, assuming you are attending school full time and another $150 per month can be added from a 'buy-up'.[20] The Post 9/11 pays for your tuition and a monthly stipend equivalent to an E-5 living allowance.[21] Right now you may be wondering what the problem is. After all, law school tuition and a stipend sounds like a deal right? The major problem is for those readers that need to obtain an undergraduate degree first.

---

[20] Ibid at

<http://www.gibill.va.gov/resources/benefits_resources/rates/CH30/ch30rates1001 12.htm> accessed 10 January 2013

[21] Ibid at

<http://www.gibill.va.gov/resources/benefits_resources/rates/CH33/Ch33rates080 112.html#MHA> accessed 10 January 2013

Undergraduate degrees cost substantially less than graduate law degrees. This combined with the fact that the Post 9/11 is treated as a living allowance and tied to a zip code is a factor to be looked at. The lower the cost of living for the area, then that means the living stipend will be less for the Post 9/11 as well. Therefore, if your school's undergrad tuition is low and located in a relatively rural area, then the value of the Post 9/11 is demonstrably lowered. Under these circumstances it would be better to have the MGIB.

The four-year undergraduate and three-year graduate law degree mean seven years of school for many of you. Your education benefits last about 36 months. This can be used for either your undergraduate degree and you could start law school with little to no debt. However, law school costs are significantly more in tuition than most state undergraduate schools.

The major danger of saving your education benefit for graduate school is that you don't know that you will actually follow through with graduate school. Life changes and you could end up with student loans from undergrad that could have been paid for. A more practical issue is that student loans for the first couple years of undergrad will not likely be capable of supporting a family, if that is needed.[22]

This is a point where total cost may be diametrically opposed to practicality with regard to using your education benefits. If you can afford to utilize your education benefits on law school, then you are likely to get more value from your benefits and owe less money in student loans when you are finished. A part-time job during undergrad may be worth the difficulty. For those of you with dependents, the issues should be clear and you should spend some extra time planning your overall financial strategy.

---

[22] U.S. Department of Education, Federal Student Aid, Loans, 'How much can I borrow?' <http://studentaid.ed.gov/types/loans/subsidized-unsubsidized#how-much-can-i-borrow> accessed 10 January 2013

For those that use part of your MGIB in undergrad and continue on to law school or use the MGIB in law school and decide to specialize in an LLM program, there is some good news. There is the potential for an additional year of benefits for you. There is an educational entitlement that is not advertised very well but is incredibly important. The VA has permitted MGIB to use their entire MGIB benefit and then transfer to the Post 9/11 benefit with up to 12 months of entitlement to be useable under the Post 9/11 regime.[23] Care should be taken to use this path. This author recommends you contact the VA to verify that the process is still being permitted under the same circumstances. Previously prior service members were loosing benefits because they were not properly counseled that the MGIB must be completely exhausted under this program or the additional, up to 12 months, entitlements may not be applied.

---

[23] United States Department of Veterans Affairs (n 20) at
<http://www.gibill.va.gov/benefits/post_911_gibill/Post911_changes.html>
accessed 10 January 2013

For general information on other military education benefits visit <www.va.gov>. If you have any questions regarding the material on the website ensure that you contact the VA before proceeding. A misunderstanding may cause you months in delays or loss of benefits.

CHAPTER IV: WHERE TO GO

Selecting a Law School

If you desire to have particular schools recommended to you, then please understand that this book will not provide such a suggestion. There are good points to many law schools regardless of their national rankings. In fact, if you look very closely, then you will see that some of the lower ranked schools are out performing ivy-league schools in certain practical areas. Take some time to decide the schools that you will be submitting your applications to. The following schools that are mentioned are intended only for use as an example in order to illustrate the subject matter of the discussion.

Where you go to law school has many factors that you should consider carefully. Are you looking to further a public service initiative? If so, then research the law school to see if public service is important to the school. Florida A&M University provides an online letter to prospective students that clearly indicate that the school supports '...diversity...and [they have a] commitment to public service'.[24] Florida A&M University has also established a prominent clinical division and many global ties for students that wish to enter the international arena.

If you have the grades, the LSAT scores and financial requirements to attend an ivy-league school, then you may desire to attend that law school in order to secure financial security and stability from the outset. Cornell, for example, has over a 98% employment rate for its law grads.[25] High level of employability is not an issue to be taken lightly.

---

[24] Florida A&M University (n 8)
<http://www.law.famu.edu/go.cfm/do/Page.View/pid/7/t/Prospective-Students> accessed 10 January 2013

[25] Business Insider (n 7)

Certain law schools have a reputation and infrastructure to produce certain specialist skill sets. American University Washington, College of Law has a Center for Human Rights and Humanitarian Law (humanitarian law is a term-of-art that means law of armed conflict or law of war) that is well equipped to develop skill sets in the human rights or humanitarian fields.[26] If you want to enter a niche field, then you should definitely look at the school's infrastructure to see if they have a developed program that will help you get what you are looking for out of a life in the legal profession. Perhaps location may be an important factor for you.

---

[26] American University Washington, College of Law, Center for Human Rights & Humanitarian Law, 'Projects' <http://www.wcl.american.edu/humright/center/projects/> accessed 10 January 2013

Location, Location, Location

Location can be an important factor in the field you want to go into. Texas law schools seem to have an energy law theme while law schools in Washington, D.C. have an international flavor. Perhaps you simply want to stay at your current home and commute to the closest law school. Either way, location is a factor to consider in your decision of choosing which law school to attend. Do not discount the convenience of having a law school within reasonable commuting distance of your current home—the key word is reasonable. Remember, time will be a commodity that you will need when you are in law school. Commuting will provide an instant and unfortunate reduction in your ability to spend time on your studies.

There is the possibility of attending a school based upon an alternative location rationale. Perhaps you simply wish to go a warm environment. Maybe you want to be as close to New York City as possible so that you can be in a large city. You could take a few years to see the beauty of California by attending law school there. Maybe you want to go to Florida and be near a beach or Disney. Location should be considered to some degree when you are considering which law school is right for you.

Late 2008 this author decided to attend law school. Out of eight applications that I sent out, over half resulted in an acceptance letter being mailed to my home near Orlando, Florida. My location choices were to move to Ohio, Virginia, or stay in Central Florida and commute to law school. My family was settled into the area and the mortgage on my home suggested that I stay in Central Florida. My choice was narrowed down to two choices, both located in Orlando, Florida. The final selection was based upon other circumstances beyond location.

Program Infrastructure

Institutional programs, connections and classes offered are factors that should weigh heavily upon selecting a law school. A strong program with relevant classes can develop you as a student to compete in a global marketplace. An institutional program that has established connections will provide you with more options to build your resume in the field that you desire to practice.

When choosing between the remaining two law schools in Orlando, the institutional programs and their connections played a massive role for me. I had a scholarship to one law school in Orlando, but the competing law school (Florida A&M University, College of Law) had an intriguing program. Florida A&M had a strong international law program with connections to the Supreme Court of Ghana, the CIA, the US Air Force, the International Criminal Tribunal for Rwanda, US Department of State and many more organizations of an international nature.[27]

---

[27] Florida A&M University, College of Law, 'Viewbook' 15-6 <http://www.law.famu.edu/download/file/viewbook/FAMU-College-of-Law-Viewbook.pdf> accessed 10 January 2013

The Center for International Law and Justice (CILJ) was the key to what I wanted out of law. Faculty in the CILJ provided an excellent supporting role in my exploration of international law. The CILJ helped to get me an internship with a US Air Force Staff Judge Advocate. The CILJ also provided the motivation I needed to study at the University of Oxford during my 2L summer.

Realistic Assessment

One of the basic factors to be considered is which schools that your record qualifies you for. Your undergraduate GPA, LSAT score, LSAT essay, personal statement and resume are some of the criteria that you will likely be judged by. Many schools have a range, generally, of GPA and LSAT scores that they begin accepting new recruits.

The LSAC has a matrix that anyone can use to calculate a general range in the form of percentage of probability that your scores have in successfully obtaining an offer of admission to basically all law schools.[28] This tool will help you formulate a strategy on securing a spot in a law school. I used a multi-pronged strategy during my application to law school.

---

[28] Law School Admission Council, 'Official Guide' <https://officialguide.lsac.org/release/OfficialGuide_Default.aspx> accessed 10 January 2013

Strategy in selecting which law schools to apply to can be simple or as complex as you wish to make it. The advice I got, and am now passing on to you, is that you should choose a couple law schools that you have a 15-35% probability of success under the LSAC calculator and you just couldn't pass up if they were to select you—a dream option. Then, select two to three schools that you have a 30-80% probability of success under the LSAC calculator and you would seriously consider and be happy to go to. Finally, choose 2-3 schools that you have 90%-100% probability of success and ensure that these options appeal to you in some of the above-mentioned factors—the sure thing. When you have all of these schools selected, do not be surprised when the application fees begin to add up. Some schools offer fee waivers for application fees. Is there a proverbial decision day that you choose between the acceptance letters? This is a complicated question.

Acceptance (hopefully) and denial letters will trickle in the mail. When you get your first acceptance letter you will have a knee-jerk reaction and want to accept immediately. If that school is your number one dream choice, then fax in your acceptance and be done with this part of the process. However, if there are other schools that you would prefer to attend that have not responded yet, then read the acceptance letter carefully for a required response date. If there is no marked response date, then contact the school and ask how much time that you have before a response is required. Normally, you should have at least two or more weeks. Mark every required response date on your calendar.

Keep in mind that a bird in the hand is worth two in the bush. If you have one or two acceptance letters, perhaps a few declination letters, but you are waiting for that one or two schools to send a response, then use common sense. The majority has already spoken and you have likely arranged your preference of schools that have replied. The one or two schools that have not replied may not accept you or may do so only after others offers of admission have lapsed. However, if you really desire to go to a specific school, then call them about five to seven days before any deadline and inform them that you have an acceptance letter from another institution that you must respond by X date and you request an expedited review, if possible, due to your fervent interest in their law school.

You may get an answer, whether you like the results is a matter for another conversation. Bottom line is to be realistic and do not let law school slip from your hands due to a lapse in time because of a failure to respond to the acceptance letter. Remember one thing as you interact with these schools, your professional reputation begins when you make first contact with them.

CHAPTER V: WHAT THE HELL DO YOU DO WHEN YOU GET THERE

General Suggestions

The essence of this short book was to provide information in order to assist the reader in a determination of whether to go to law school and to help show how that could be accomplished. This chapter will be limited as it is outside of the primary scope of this book. However, key points will be addressed and should not be discounted due to the brevity of this section or chapter.

Many law schools have a mandatory legal writing and research course. If so, then feel free to skip to the next section. If not, then you will need to figure it out yourself. The ability to pull cases and journal articles, both manually in the library and electronically on Westlaw, Lexis, Hein Online or other legal search tool is invaluable. Take the time to find the librarian and ask how to pull a case or journal article and do this as early as possible.

Contrary to what many people say in their first year of law school about grades don't matter, just graduate. This has some truth, but in the larger scheme of things this will set you up for failure. Your first job offer will be based on your grades. Should you decide to specialize in an area of law by obtaining an LLM degree, they will assess you by your grades. Nearly every position you could think of will, for your first job, judge you by your transcripts as much as anything else. Therefore, you should give your complete effort from the beginning.

Most law schools are based on a grading curve. This means that X% will get an 'A' grade and Y% will get an 'F' grade. The school that you attend will likely have its grading scale posted, be aware if you are going to an institution that sets the grading curve low—especially in the first year. This creates a higher danger of failure in the program and may harm your opportunities when applying for employment after law school. Treat law school as if you want to succeed, not simply to make it through.

Find a way to stand out from the rest of your class. Get on the Law Review, take on internships during the summer locally or travel to a key area, study abroad with a top-notch school, publish an article or become a research fellow. Do what ever you have to do in order to stand out in some manner. When you finally interview, your employer will want to have something on your resume to talk about.

Poor Structure, Grammar or Just No Clue How to Put Legal Writing Together

So you have made it to law school and now your writing is considered deficient. Don't panic, poor sentence structure and grammar are fixable. The down side is that you will need to work extra hard and read a little more as well. For sentence structure and grammar I recommend you pick up a copy of 'The Elements of Style' by Strunk and White.[29]

---

[29] William Strunk Jr, E.B. White, 'The Elements of Style' (4th ed 2009 Pearson Education)

Having trouble with essays? Your school should set you down and explain the IRAC, UDW, CRAC or the school's other preferred method of addressing essays. If not, then this short book is your best friend for this section alone. We will briefly look at the IRAC method of answering essays. First the 'I' means Issue, as in you state 'the issue is whether Pam committed a battery on Danny'. The 'R' stands for Rule, as in you state 'the rule is that a battery must be intentional, there must be harmful or offensive touching to the person of another and there must be harm'. The 'A' stands for Analysis, as in you apply the facts to the rule by stating 'Pam punched Danny, another person, in the face three times breaking his nose. Pam intentionally punched Danny, the voluntariness can be shown by the fact she punched him three times. The harm was that Danny's nose was broken.' You demonstrated that all elements of the rule were met with the facts. This brings us to the 'C' that stands for Conclusion. All elements of battery were established as committed by Pam, we now state 'therefore, Pam committed a battery'.

For the Florida Bar Exam I used the UDW technique. This is a short analytical tool that is great for racehorse type exams. This method is simply Under [the law], Does [this outcome result], When [these facts happen]?[30] This should give you a couple tools to work with but you will need to fine-tune your use of them. Academic writing is another beast in itself.

Academic writing can prove to be an issue. You are expected to use a strange hybrid of analysis similar to the above methods but tied to a more cogent framework. For further information I refer you to 'Academic Legal Writing: Law Review Articles, Student Notes, Seminar Papers, and Getting on Law Review'.[31]

---

[30] Legalwriting.net, 'Issue statements: under-does-when' (2007) <http://www.utexas.edu/law/faculty/wschiess/legalwriting/2007/05/issue-statements-under-does-when.html> accessed 10 January 2013

[31] Eugene Volokh, 'Academic Legal Writing: Law Review Articles, Student Notes, Seminar Papers, and Getting on Law Review' (3rd ed 2007 Foundation Press)

Final Remarks

Congratulations on making it through this brief guide. You have been introduced to the negative aspects of the legal profession and are still interested. At least I assume you are still interested if you are continuing to read. This is an achievement that you can do. Prior service members have a strong drive and are normally well disciplined. You will succeed if you put forth a full effort. When you begin to feel overwhelmed, just think of all that you accomplished in the military. Then, tell yourself to drink water, change your socks, take an Ibuprofen and drive on. Good luck!

BIBLIOGRAPHY

Books

William Strunk Jr, E.B. White, 'The Elements of Style' (4th ed 2009 Pearson Education)

Eugene Volokh, 'Academic Legal Writing: Law Review Articles, Student Notes, Seminar Papers, and Getting on Law Review' (3rd ed 2007 Foundation Press)

Web Accessed Materials

American Bar Association, Section of Legal Education and Admissions to the Bar, 'Basic Overview' <http://www.americanbar.org/groups/legal_education/resources/bar_admissions/basic_overview.html> accessed 9 January 2013

American University Washington, College of Law, Center for Human Rights & Humanitarian Law, 'Projects' <http://www.wcl.american.edu/humright/center/projects/> accessed 10 January 2013

Associate's Mind, 'How to Juggle a Family and Law School (or a Law Firm)' <http://associatesmind.com/2011/06/23/how-to-juggle-a-family-and-law-school-or-a-law-firm/> accessed 9 January 2013

Business Insider: Law and Order, 'The 20 Most Expensive Law Schools in America' (2012) accessed 9 January 2013

Capital University, Law School, 'Family Support Services' <http://law.capital.edu/Family_Support_Services/> accessed 9 January 2013

Central Intelligence Agency, 'Career Opportunities' <https://www.cia.gov/careers/opportunities/analytical/view-jobs.html> accessed 9 January 2013

Defense Intelligence Agency, 'Careers' <http://www.dia.mil/careers/> accessed 9 January 2013

The Federal Circuit Bar Association, Bench & Bar, 'The Scholarship Series' <http://www.fedcirbar.org/olc/pub/LVFC/cpages/misc/scholar.jsp> accessed 9 January 2013

FinAid, The Smart Student Guide to Financial Aid, 'Public Service
Loan Forgiveness'
<http://www.finaid.org/loans/publicservice.phtml> accessed 10
January 2013

Florida A&M University, College of Law,
    ——Prospective Students, 'Tuition and Fees' <http://www.
    law.famu.edu/go.cfm/do/Page.View/pid/18/t/Tuition-and-
    Fees> accessed 9 January 2013

    ——<http://www.law.famu.edu/go.cfm/do/Page.View/
    pid/7/t/Prospective-Students> accessed 10 January 2013

    —— 'Viewbook' 15-6 <http://www.law.famu.edu/
    download/file/viewbook/FAMU-College-of-Law-
    Viewbook.pdf> accessed 10 January 2013

Law School Admission Council, 'Official Guide'
<https://officialguide.lsac.org/ release/OfficialGuide_Default.aspx>
accessed 10 January 2013

Legalwriting.net, 'Issue statements: under-does-when' (2007)
<http://www.utexas.edu/law/faculty/wschiess/legalwriting/2007/05/i
ssue-statements-under-does-when.html> accessed 10 January 2013

National Security Agency, Central Security Service, 'Careers' <http://www.nsa.gov/careers/career_fields/intela.shtml> accessed 9 January 2013

The New York Times, Business Day, 'The Two-Track Lawyer Market' (26 July 2010) <http://economix.blogs.nytimes.com/ 2010/07/26/the-two-track-lawyer-market/> accessed 9 January 2013

United Nations, 'Careers' <https://careers.un.org/lbw/Home.aspx> accessed 9 January 2013

United States Department of Justice, 'Legal Careers' <http://www.justice.gov/careers/legal/> accessed 9 January 2013

United States Department of State, Careers Representing America, 'Diplomats in Residence Location Map' <http://careers.state.gov/engage/dir.html> accessed 10 January 2013

United States Department of Veterans Affairs (n 20) at <http://www.gibill.va.gov/benefits/post_911_gibill/Post911_changes .html> accessed 10 January 2013

University of Kentucky, College of Law, Tuition and Residency, 'Tuition, Fees and Expenses' <http://www.law.uky.edu/index.php?pid=154> accessed 9 January 2013

www.ingramcontent.com/pod-product-compliance
Lightning Source LLC
Chambersburg PA
CBHW070612290526
45790CB00002B/887